William Henry Seward

Senator and Statesman

Colonial Leaders

Lord Baltimore
English Politician and Colonist

Benjamin Banneker
American Mathematician and Astronomer

Sir William Berkeley
Governor of Virginia

William Bradford
Governor of Plymouth Colony

Jonathan Edwards
Colonial Religious Leader

Benjamin Franklin
American Statesman, Scientist, and Writer

Anne Hutchinson
Religious Leader

Cotton Mather
Author, Clergyman, and Scholar

Increase Mather
Clergyman and Scholar

James Oglethorpe
Humanitarian and Soldier

William Penn
Founder of Democracy

Sir Walter Raleigh
English Explorer and Author

Caesar Rodney
American Patriot

John Smith
English Explorer and Colonist

Miles Standish
Plymouth Colony Leader

Peter Stuyvesant
Dutch Military Leader

George Whitefield
Clergyman and Scholar

Roger Williams
Founder of Rhode Island

John Winthrop
Politician and Statesman

John Peter Zenger
Free Press Advocate

Revolutionary War Leaders

John Adams
Second U.S. President

Samuel Adams
Patriot

Ethan Allen
Revolutionary Hero

Benedict Arnold
Traitor to the Cause

John Burgoyne
British General

George Rogers Clark
American General

Lord Cornwallis
British General

Thomas Gage
British General

King George III
English Monarch

Nathanael Greene
Military Leader

Nathan Hale
Revolutionary Hero

Alexander Hamilton
First U.S. Secretary of the Treasury

John Hancock
President of the Continental Congress

Patrick Henry
American Statesman and Speaker

William Howe
British General

John Jay
First Chief Justice of the Supreme Court

Thomas Jefferson
Author of the Declaration of Independence

John Paul Jones
Father of the U.S. Navy

Thaddeus Kosciuszko
Polish General and Patriot

Lafayette
French Freedom Fighter

James Madison
Father of the Constitution

Francis Marion
The Swamp Fox

James Monroe
American Statesman

Thomas Paine
Political Writer

Molly Pitcher
Heroine

Paul Revere
American Patriot

Betsy Ross
American Patriot

Baron Von Steuben
American General

George Washington
First U.S. President

Anthony Wayne
American General

Famous Figures of the Civil War Era

John Brown
Abolitionist

Jefferson Davis
Confederate President

Frederick Douglass
Abolitionist and Author

Stephen A. Douglas
Champion of the Union

David Farragut
Union Admiral

Ulysses S. Grant
Military Leader and President

Stonewall Jackson
Confederate General

Joseph E. Johnston
Confederate General

Robert E. Lee
Confederate General

Abraham Lincoln
Civil War President

George Gordon Meade
Union General

George McClellan
Union General

William Henry Seward
Senator and Statesman

Philip Sheridan
Union General

William Sherman
Union General

Edwin Stanton
Secretary of War

Harriet Beecher Stowe
Author of Uncle Tom's Cabin

James Ewell Brown Stuart
Confederate General

Sojourner Truth
Abolitionist, Suffragist, and Preacher

Harriet Tubman
Leader of the Underground Railroad

William Henry Seward

Senator and Statesman

Michael Burgan

Arthur M. Schlesinger, jr.
Senior Consulting Editor

Chelsea House Publishers

Philadelphia

CHELSEA HOUSE PUBLISHERS
Editor-in-Chief Sally Cheney
Director of Production Kim Shinners
Production Manager Pamela Loos
Art Director Sara Davis
Production Editor Diann Grasse

Staff for *WILLIAM HENRY SEWARD*
Editor Sally Cheney
Associate Art Director Takeshi Takahashi
Series Design Keith Trego
Layout by D&G Limited. LLC

The Chelsea House World Wide Web address is
http://www.chelseahouse.com

First Printing
1 3 5 7 9 8 6 4 2

Library of Congress Cataloging-in-Publication Data

Burgan, Michael.
    William Henry Seward : senator and statesman / Michael Burgan.
       p. cm. — (Famous figures of the Civil War era)
    Includes bibliographical references and index.
    ISBN 0-7910-6418-2 (alk. paper) — ISBN 0-7910-6419-0 (pbk. : alk. paper)
      1. Seward, William Henry, 1801-1872—Juvenile literature. 2. Cabinet
    officers—United States—Biography—Juvenile literature. 3. Statesmen—
    United States—Biography—Juvenile literature. 4. Legislators—United
    States—Biography—Juvenile literature. 5. United States. Congress. Senate—
    Biography—Juvenile literature. 6. United States—Politics and government—
    1861-1865—Juvenile literature. 7. United States—Foreign relations—1861-
    1865—Juvenile literature. [1. Seward, William Henry, 1801-1872. 2.
    Statesmen. 3. United States—Politics and government—1861-1865.] I. Title.
    II. Series.

E415.9.S4 B87 2001
973.7'092—dc21
[B]   2001028764

Publisher's Note: In Colonial, Revolutionary War, and Civil War Era
America, there were no standard rules for spelling, punctuation,
capitalization, or grammar. Some of the quotations that appear in
the Colonial Leaders, Revolutionary War Leaders, and Famous
Figures of the Civil War Era series come from original documents
and letters written during this time in history. Original quotations
reflect writing inconsistencies of the period.

Contents

Men, women, and children were taken from Africa and brought to the United States. They were then sold to plantation owners in the South. Slaves worked for little or no money in the fields and homes of their owners, and they had no rights or freedoms. This arrangement benefited the plantation owners and was an important part of the Southern economy. Plantation owners could operate their farms with very few expenses.

Preparing
for Politics

William Henry Seward's life began in a farming community in Orange County, New York. Born on May 16, 1801, Harry, as he was called as a boy, was the fourth child of Samuel and Mary Seward. There would eventually be six children in their family.

Samuel was a doctor and a farmer in the village of Florida. He also served as a judge and worked as a merchant, which helped him provide for his family. Mary had a good sense of humor and was known for her desire to always seed the truth.

The Seward family had a strong interest in politics. While William was still a toddler, his father was elected to the New York senate. There, Mr. Seward helped write laws for the state. Early in William's life, Mr. Seward decided his son should go to college and study law.

William attended the village school and then Farmers' Hall Academy. In class, he worked hard and made many friends. "My daily studies," William later wrote, "began at five in the morning, and closed at nine at night." When he wasn't studying, he helped out on the farm.

At age 15, William entered Union College in Schenectady, New York. At that time, students did not attend high schools, and they entered college at an early age. At college, William once again had an easy time making friends. A family friend who visited him at Union wrote, "The confidence which he has in himself and [his] ease of manners [make] him quite pleasing."

William sometimes got into trouble at Union. He once refused to return to a class because he thought a teacher had treated him unfairly. The school principal apologized to William, and then

William apologized to the teacher. Sometime later, William owed money to a local tailor, who sent the bill to Mr. Seward. William's father refused to pay it, and William could not afford to. William decided to leave school and head to Georgia with a classmate. His father was angry, though he still loved his son enough to send him $100. William gladly took the money–but he did not return to Union.

As a boy, William enjoyed having a good time with his friends and playing pranks. William also enjoyed playing cards. In college, he was called from a card game to attend church services. William stuck the cards in his hat and rushed into the church. Inside, his hat fell off, and the cards came tumbling out. William kept his love of cards throughout his life. According to one story, he made the deal to buy Alaska while in the middle of a card game.

Early in 1819, William found a job as a teacher in Putnam County, Georgia. He taught spelling, math, languages, and geography. His career as a teacher did not last long. But his time in Georgia influenced George's entire life. He saw for the first time how slavery was practiced in the South. By June 1819, he was back in New

York. In the fall he returned to college and graduated the next spring.

For a time, the Sewards had three slaves who lived with the family. Still, William later recalled that his parents "never uttered an expression that could tend to make me think that the negro was inferior to the white person." At times, the Seward children helped teach the slave children how to read.

During William's childhood, some Northern states had already ended slavery. More states would slowly follow. After 1799, slave owners in New York had to free their slaves when they reached their twenties. By 1827 all New York slaves had their freedom.

Slavery was different in the South. More people owned slaves there than in the North. Some Southern slave owners had large farms called **plantations**. They needed many slaves to help plant and pick cotton and other crops. Slaves often lived apart from their white owners. Teaching slaves to read, as William once did, was often a crime. In Georgia, William learned how terrible slavery could be. The result, he later wrote, "was to confirm and strengthen the opinions I already [had against] slavery."

Slavery, however, was not William's first concern. He was eager to practice law. He studied it after leaving Union, and in 1822 he became a lawyer. William accepted a job working with Judge Elijah Miller of Auburn, New York. Within two years, William became part of Miller's family, too. In October 1824, the young lawyer married Frances Miller, the judge's daughter.

William and Frances lived with the elder Millers, and William became an active citizen of Auburn. His law work went well. Outside of the courtroom, be joined the local volunteer army, called a **militia**. He also became involved in politics. During the election of 1824, William supported John Quincy Adams for president.

In the United States "electors" from each state actually choose the president. These citizens take part in what is called an electoral vote. In each state, **candidates** from different parties have electors who promise to vote for them. But first the voters decide which group of electors will represent their state. The candidate who gets the most support in this popular vote then wins a state's electoral votes.

In 1824, four men ran for president. Adams won the most popular votes. Andrew Jackson won more electoral votes than Adams did, but did not have enough votes to become president. When this happens, the members of the House of Representatives choose the president. That year, the House elected Adams as president.

But in 1828 Adams lost his reelection bid to Andrew Jackson. During that election year, William became even more involved in politics. He joined the Anti-Masonic Party, which had just recently appeared in New York. Members of the party opposed an organization called the Masons. The Anti-Masons had support from farmers, craftsmen, and others who believed the Masons controlled America.

John Quincy Adams ran against Andrew Jackson and won the election to become the country's sixth president. He served from 1825 to 1829.

Andrew Jackson was the seventh president, serving from 1829 to 1837.

The first Masonic lodges, or clubs, began in England early in the 18th century. The Masons kept the details of their club secret. The first members were mostly stonemasons, men who built with stones. Over time, however, men with other careers also joined. Some of these members were lawyers and other powerful people in society.

Masonry soon spread among the American colonies. Famous Masons in America included Benjamin Franklin and George Washington. In general, the Masons strongly supported the American Revolution. But in the 19th century, some Americans thought Masons had too much control over politics and the legal system. This upset some people–including William. But William had another reason for joining the Anti-Masons. In New York, he believed, it was the only party strong enough to challenge President Jackson and the Democratic Party. Many other Americans joined the Anti-Masons for the same reason.

The Anti-Masonic party spread quickly across the Northeast. At first William did not want to join the party. He still supported Adams's party, the National Republican Party. Many members of this party, however, were joining the Anti-Masons. Williams thought most of these men were "honest, earnest, vigorous, and intelligent." He began to write speeches for the party's politicians in New York. Slowly he became a full supporter of the Anti-Masonic cause.

William spoke out against Masonry, calling it a threat to liberty. In 1830, he attended a state **convention** for Anti-Masons. William played an active role. He helped convince the members that the party should work for reform in New York. In particular, he backed new canals and an end to wasteful government spending. Later in the year, William went to Philadelphia for the party's national convention. He spoke about the party's rising strength.

William was friendly with the Anti-Masons' party leaders in New York. They asked him to run for the state senate, and William won the race. At the end of 1830, William took a stage-coach to Albany, ready to begin the next stage of his public life.

This advertisement for the abolition of slavery was made for the Antislavery Society, which was formed in 1831. The poster shows African Americans going from freedom in their country to slavery in the United States. It also depicts the conflict between slavery and the right to liberty.

Senator and Governor

William Henry Seward officially became a New York state senator on January 4, 1831. Short and boyish, he looked younger than his 29 years. At first William felt out of place around the other senators. He later wrote, "My tongue [stuck] to the roof of my mouth whenever I thought of taking the floor." But William was intelligent, and he wanted to succeed in politics. He devoted himself to his new job.

William was one of seven Anti-Masonic senators that year. The leader of the New York Anti-Masons was Thurlow Weed. He and William had first met in 1824. Weed was a journalist and one of the founders of the Anti-Masonic Party in New York. He had strongly supported William's run for the senate, and the two men became close friends. In the years ahead, Weed would continue to help William's political career.

As a senator, William worked on issues he felt strongly about. He wanted to reform the state's prisons and have separate jails for women. He also supported plans to start new railroads. William firmly believed that railroads were for the public's good, and the government should run them.

While William worked in Albany, many Americans were stunned by an event in Virginia. In August 1831, a slave named Nat Turner led a **revolt**. Almost 200 people—black and white—died during this slave revolt. William later wrote that Turner's rebellion was America's "first practical and solemn warning against the error of [continuing] African slavery." After the revolt, William saw clearly "the necessity of a peaceful reform of that great evil."

In 1832, President Jackson ran for reelection. William and other Anti-Masons supported William Wirt. Jackson, however, won easily. The Anti-Masons were disappointed with the results, but William went back to work in the Senate. During his time at Albany, William kept working as a lawyer. He also found time to travel, taking his first trip to Europe. When he returned to America, William saw that his party was about to crumble.

Both the Anti-Masonic and National Republican parties in New York were losing support. Many members of both parties came together to form a new party, the Whigs. The party members held many different beliefs, but they united over their dislike of President Jackson. The party's name came from the Whig Party in Great Britain, which opposed the British **monarchy**. American Whigs thought that President Jackson ruled as if he were a king. The Whigs hoped to limit Jackson's power.

William and his friend Weed quickly became important Whigs in New York. In the fall of

1834, Weed backed William as the party's candidate for governor. William fought hard, telling voters he would reform state government. No one, however, expected the Whigs to win, and William lost the race by about 11,000 votes.

After his loss, William wrote to Weed, "I shall not suffer any unhappiness in returning to private life." William went back to Auburn and his law practice. He worked long hours and his business grew. He also had a chance to spend time with Frances and his two young sons, Frederick and Augustus. But William never turned completely away from politics.

He also never forgot about the evils of slavery. On a trip to Virginia, he saw young slaves who would later be sold across the South. They were treated like animals raised to be sold at a market. William wrote his sister, "I often think over the wrongs of this injured race."

During local elections in 1837, the Whig Party did well in New York. William soon thought again about running for governor, and

This slave sale was held outdoors in Montgomery, Alabama.

once again his party made him its candidate. This time the outcome was different. In the November 1838 election, William won by about 10,000 votes.

William soon moved back to Albany to prepare for his new position. On New Year's Day, 1839, he was sworn in as governor. He turned to familiar issues: prison reform, railroads, and

Governors in the early part of the 19th century often had parties when they first took office. They opened up their homes so citizens could stop by and say hello. In January 1839, William hosted one of these parties for New Yorkers.

William put out tables with turkey, ham, beef, cheese, crackers, and wine. Bands played music, and people streamed through the house all day. William's young son Augustus was at the party. He described the scene in a letter to his aunt: "Pa come home and let about 2 or 3 thousand people in the house and they crowded in so fast that they upset one of the tables."

education. William often turned to Weed for help. The governor deeply trusted his longtime friend.

During his time as governor, William spoke out several times about slavery and the rights of free African Americans. Although slavery was now illegal in the North, some people there still had strong **prejudice** against blacks. In the South, any talk of ending or even limiting slavery brought an angry reaction. William had to take a careful stand on race issues. Personally, he believed slavery was wrong and African Americans deserved equal rights with whites. His wife Frances held even stronger views on ending slavery. But as a politician, William did not want to say too much about slavery that might offend voters.

Still, William did take public stands against slavery. Late in 1839, three African Americans from New York tried to help a slave escape from Virginia. Helping a slave escape was a crime in the South. The escape failed, but the governor of Virginia still demanded that the three New Yorkers be sent to court in Virginia. William refused to send the men. He took the same position with another case involving Georgia. He refused to send an escaped slave back to that state.

Southerners began to speak out strongly against William. So did some members of his own party. But **abolitionists** supported William's actions. They had formed the Liberty Party to fight slavery. In 1842 some party members asked William to run as their candidate for the U.S. Congress. He declined. The abolitionists, however, saw that William was one political leader who might help their cause.

"The Tragic Prelude," a mural by John Steuart
Curry, is displayed in the Topeka, Kansas, State
Capitol. It depicts abolitionist John Brown's life-long
fight against slavery. He was hanged for his role in
the takeover of a U.S. armory at Harpers Ferry,
Virginia.

In January 1843, William left the office of
governor and returned to Auburn. Once again,
he prepared to practice law. His law practice
grew quickly, and William traveled across New

York. His family had grown–he now had three sons, and a daughter was born in 1844. Frances and several African-American servants ran the household as William took on legal cases.

Two of those cases upset many people in Auburn and across New York. Both involved free African Americans on trial for murder. Henry Wyatt was already in jail when he was accused of killing another prisoner. William Freeman was accused of killing a farmer and his family. In each case, William was sure the two men were suffering from mental illness. His work with prison reform had shown him that the mentally ill did not receive fair treatment in the courts or in jail. William was also concerned about the legal rights of blacks.

Early in 1846, Wyatt went on trial, but the jury could not reach a verdict. In a second trial, Wyatt was found guilty. Later in the year, William was still deciding whether he should take the Freeman case. He wrote a letter to Weed and noted that the people opposed his defending Freeman. "But I shall do my duty," William wrote. "I care not whether I am to be ever forgiven for it or not."

The Freeman trial started in July. William argued that Freeman was innocent because of insanity. Other members of his family had suffered mental illnesses. Freeman had also once received a blow to the head that damaged his hearing and his skull. In the courtroom, Freeman often seemed confused. William had doctors testify that Freeman was insane. The state, however, had its own doctors. They claimed Freeman was sane and knew he was committing murder. The state wanted Freeman to hang.

In his closing remarks, William told the jury it should not rule against Freeman because of his color. "There is not a *white* man, or a *white* woman," he said, "who would not have been dismissed long since from the perils of such a [trial] . . ." But William's defense was not enough. The jury found Freeman guilty, and he was sentenced to hang. William appealed the case to the U.S. Supreme Court. The nation's highest court ruled that Freeman did not receive a fair trial. The Court ordered a new one. Unfortunately, Freeman died in 1847 while waiting for that trial to begin.

William said that the Wyatt and Freeman trials left him "exhausted in mind and body." He had once hoped that by taking the cases, he might improve the legal rights of blacks in New York. That effort failed. But William did win wider fame for himself, and he remained dedicated to the cause of helping African Americans.

CHARLESTON
MERCURY
EXTRA:

Passed unanimously at 1.15 o'clock, P. M. December
20th, 1860.

AN ORDINANCE

To dissolve the Union between the State of South Carolina and
other States united with her under the compact entitled " The
Constitution of the United States of America."

We, the People of the State of South Carolina, in Convention assembled, do declare and ordain, and
it is hereby declared and ordained,

That the Ordinance adopted by us in Convention, on the twenty-third day of May, in the
year of our Lord one thousand seven hundred and eighty-eight, whereby the Constitution of the
United States of America was ratified, and also, all Acts and parts of Acts of the General
Assembly of this State, ratifying amendments of the said Constitution, are hereby repealed;
and that the union now subsisting between South Carolina and other States, under the name of
"The United States of America," is hereby dissolved.

THE
UNION
IS
DISSOLVED!

This broadside announces South Carolina's secession from the Union in 1861. More Southern states followed, forming the Confederate States of America. The Civil War between the North and South over slavery would soon begin.

National Politics

As William practiced law, he also followed political events. By 1848, he was calling the Democratic Party the party of slavery. The Democrats, especially in the South, supported the spread of slavery into new states. Other Whigs did not always agree with William on slavery and other issues.

Being popular was not an issue—unless William wanted to return to politics. And by 1848, he did. He made many speeches and was one of the leaders of the Whig Party. During one speaking tour, he met an Illinois lawyer named Abraham Lincoln. The two men had similar feelings about slavery. One night they spent many hours talking, not knowing they would work closely together in years to come.

Some Whigs thought William should be the party's candidate for vice president in 1848. Instead, he focused on becoming a U.S. senator for New York. At the time, the members of the legislature in each state chose U.S. senators. In the New York legislature, some Whigs opposed William. They disliked his strong feelings against slavery. But on February 6, 1849, William won an easy victory. He promised he would not do anything that might harm the Union as he worked against slavery.

Keeping the United States together was a concern. In the South, some politicians talked about a state's right to secede, or break away from the other states. As more Northerners talked about limiting or ending slavery, more Southerners talked about **secession**. William wanted to end slavery, but he wanted all the states to remain united.

William arrived in Washington, D.C., in November and entered the Senate the next month. Almost immediately, a few Southern Democrats attacked his views on slavery. None of the other Whigs rose to defend him. William told a friend, "I am _alone_ all _alone_ in the Senate."

Early in 1850, Senator Henry Clay of Kentucky called for a **compromise** between those who supported slavery and those who attacked it. He said California should join the Union as a free state–slavery would be illegal there. In other western lands, Congress would let the people decide whether or not they wanted slavery. In March, William spoke out against Clay's plan.

William did not want slavery in the western territories. He also did not want a compromise. Trying to protect slavery, William said, was wrong. He said, "There is a higher law than the Constitution," meaning that slavery was against the laws of God. William thought the Union could be preserved while ending slavery.

William was not an abolitionist. He did not want to end slavery immediately, at any cost. He said, "I will adopt none but lawful, constitutional,

and peaceful means, to secure even that end."
Still, to many Americans William seemed liked a
radical after his "higher law" speech. Newspapers in both the North and South attacked his
position, as did members of his own party. Even
his friend Weed had problems with the speech.
From a political view, it was not wise to attack a
law supported by powerful Whigs. These
included Daniel Webster, a senator from Massachusetts, and President Zachary Taylor.

Slowly, however, William won some praise
for his speech. It became the most famous
speech of his career. He and his friends sent out
about 100,000 copies of the speech and it
appeared in many newspapers. William seemed
to enjoy his new position as a famous politician.

Despite William's speech, Clay's Compromise of 1850 became law. The next few years,
William did not speak out as strongly against
slavery. During the elections of 1852, the Whigs
were trying not to stir up voters on this issue.
The party chose General Winfield Scott as its

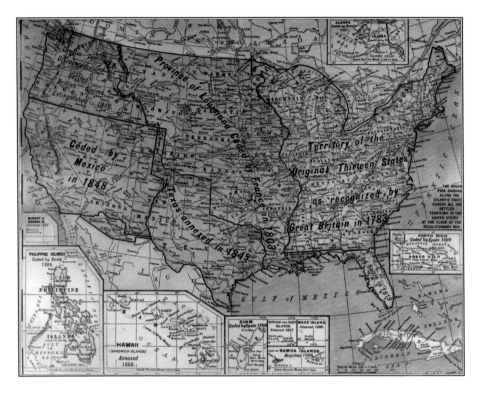

Many Americans believed in "Manifest Destiny." This was the concept that the United States was destined to reach from the Atlantic to the Pacific Ocean. This map shows how the United States looked in the 1800s. As the country grew, the question of whether or not new states would be free states, or allow slavery, became important.

candidate for president. He lost to Democrat Franklin K. Pierce.

The Whig Party began to decline in membership. Southern Whigs disliked William and other

Northerners who opposed slavery. Northern Whigs disagreed with each other on slavery, the role of immigrants in America, and economic issues. The party could not survive for long.

In 1854 another important law was debated in the U.S. Senate. The Kansas-Nebraska Act called for ending a previous law that limited slavery in some western territories. The act also created the territories of Kansas and Nebraska and let the residents there decide if they wanted slavery.

William opposed the Kansas-Nebraska Act, and once again he gave a notable speech in the Senate. The bill, he said, showed a conflict "between truth and error, between right and wrong." Most legislators, however, supported the bill, and President Pierce signed it into law.

After the Kansas-Nebraska Act, American politics changed dramatically. New parties emerged. Some were tied to the issue of slavery. Another party, the Know-Nothings, formed to oppose immigrants. One older party, the Free-Soilers, also gained some strength. This party opposed the spread of slavery in the West. In New York, William ran again as a Whig and won reelection to the Senate. Soon however, William joined a new party–the Republicans.

The Republican Party formed in 1854. It appealed to former Whigs, Free Soilers, and others who opposed slavery. William did not join right away. He wanted to remain loyal to the Whigs. But by the summer of 1855 he realized the Republicans were a more powerful political force.

William spoke for the Republicans in New York, calling for an end to slavery in new territories. In the Senate, he and other Republicans sided with antislavery forces in Kansas. About 5,000 citizens of Missouri had come into Kansas and set up a government that favored slavery. Kansans who opposed slavery then set up their own government. The conflict in Kansas was one example of the growing anger over slavery. Seward warned that the United States could not safely grow if Americans were "faithless to the interests of universal freedom."

By early 1856 the Republicans saw that more people in the North were against slavery. They planned to run their first candidate for president and **nominated** John C. Frémont. He was an explorer who had fought bravely during the Mexican-American War. In the election, Frémont won New York, the New England states, and a few states farther west. Democrat James Buchanan won all the Southern states and some in the Midwest. He earned enough electoral votes to win the election. Clearly, the United States was dividing on the issue of slavery.

For the next few years, William was active in the Senate. He joined the Foreign Relations Committee, which studied America's issues with other countries. But in 1858, slavery was still a hot topic in Kansas. Antislavery forces were upset over the *Dred Scott* case. In 1857 the U.S. Supreme Court had ruled on a case brought by a slave named Dred Scott. The court said slaves were not U.S. citizens and did not have legal rights. In the Senate, William opposed slavery in

Kansas and the *Dred Scott* decision.

In October 1858, William gave a speech in Rochester, New York. Slavery, he said, harmed democracy. Only free citizens could keep a free government. The conflict between slavery and freedom was **"irrepressible,"** or impossible to control. If slavery won this battle, William said, he would not want to live in America. "I shall never be a **denizen** of a State where men and women are reared as cattle, and bought and sold as merchandise."

William Seward opposed slavery but did not criticize others who had different beliefs. This was not true with Charles Sumner. An abolitionist senator from Massachusetts, Sumner in 1856 spoke against the people of South Carolina and one of their senators for supporting slavery.

William had read the speech before Sumner gave it. He warned Sumner to leave out some of his harsher words, but Sumner refused. A few days after giving the speech, a congressman from South Carolina attacked Sumner. This bloody attack hinted on the violence that was to come over the issue of slavery.

In 1859, William spent almost six months traveling in Europe. While he was away, an abolitionist named John Brown tried to lead a

Republican Abraham Lincoln was elected as the 16th president of the United States in November 1860. The Southern states did not approve of Lincoln's policies on slavery. Before Lincoln's inauguration in March 1861, Southern states had already begun to secede from the Union.

slave rebellion in Virginia. The effort failed, and Brown was killed. William returned home to learn that some Southern senators thought he was somehow involved in Brown's raid of an army arsenal. The charge was not true, but William faced growing hatred because of it.

The next year, William once again thought about running for president. Early in 1860, he gave a popular speech defending the Republican Party. Some Democrats claimed the Republicans were destroying the country by attacking slavery. William argued that his party wanted to save the Union.

Some Republicans thought William spoke out too strongly against slavery. The party wanted someone who had been less vocal about ending slavery. He had also been hard on the Know–Nothings. Many of them would vote for a Republican candidate–unless it were William.

At their 1860 convention, the Republicans considered both William and Abraham Lincoln to be their candidate. After several close votes, Lincoln finally won. William told his friends, "Well, Mr. Lincoln will be elected and has some of the qualities that make a good president."

Shown here are army tents outside of Richmond, Virginia, which was the capital of the Confederate States of America. The Confederacy was made up of the Southern states that seceded from the United States.

Slavery Divides the Nation

William Seward and Abraham Lincoln had similar beliefs on slavery. Both wanted to stop the spread of slavery in America's new territories. Both also believed the nation could not be allowed to split apart over slavery. These shared ideas made it easier for the two men to work together.

William traveled in the West, making speeches for Lincoln and the Republicans. Lincoln faced a difficult race to become president. Four major parties had nominated candidates. The Democrats split into Northern and Southern halves and nominated two candidates, Stephen Douglas and John C. Breck-inridge. The new Constitutional Union Party nominated John Bell. The race was devoted to the issue of slavery and whether the United States would survive the discord.

On Election Day 1860, the Northern and Western states solidly supported Lincoln. The popular vote was fairly close, but Lincoln easily won the electoral votes. Leaders in some Southern states feared that Lincoln and the Republicans would try to end slavery everywhere. Most Southerners believed each state had the right to choose if it should have slavery. They did not want the national government telling them what to do. They also believed their economies would crumble if slavery were abolished.

Lincoln told the Southerners he did not want to end slavery where it already existed. William repeated this message in the Senate. In January, he gave a speech outlining plans to keep the South satisfied. He also attacked the idea of splitting apart the United States over slavery. He later said, "With the loss of Union all would be lost. Now, therefore, I speak [only] for Union, striving if possible to save it peaceably."

By now, most Southern states were preparing to secede. South Carolina had already acted, and others were ready to join it. William received letters from concerned Americans. They pleaded with him to find a way to save the Union.

William now had a new role in government. Lincoln chose him to be secretary of state. This member of the president's **cabinet** leads the U.S. Department of State. The secretary of state handles America's relations with foreign countries. But Lincoln also wanted William's help on other matters. As a national political figure, William could play a role in the growing crisis over secession.

On February 8, 1861, the seceding Southern states voted to create a new nation. They called it the Confederate States of America (CSA). Around the same time, William led a meeting in Washington that tried to find a peaceful end to the problem. He hoped to convince the **border states** to stay in the Union. These states allowed slavery, but bordered Northern states that did not. So far, all the states that had seceded were deep in the South.

Lincoln was sworn in as president on March 4. William reviewed the president's first speech and suggested a few changes. Lincoln knew the country faced a war over secession. He stated again that he did not want to end slavery in the South. He also said the secession was illegal. He considered the Southern states still part of the Union, and he would enforce the Constitution there. "In doing this," he said, "there needs to be no bloodshed or violence, and there shall be none unless it be forced upon the national authority."

For several weeks, Lincoln and his cabinet debated what to do. William still hoped to avoid a war, but that soon became impossible. In April, Lincoln sent supplies to Fort Sumter, in Charleston, South Carolina. The fort was still under Union control. On April 12, 1861, before the supplies reached the fort, the Confederacy attacked and the Civil War began.

William hoped the war would be short. His son Frederick was with his father in Washington. He wrote to his mother, "Father is quite confident the whole storm will blow over." But William also knew the North had to take the war seriously. Soon he was working to get guns and supplies for the Union forces.

Willliam almost did not serve as secretary of state. Early in 1861, he began to feel he did not have Abraham Lincoln's support. He had hoped to do more to help Lincoln choose his cabinet. On March 2, William wrote a letter to Lincoln saying he would not become secretary of state. Two days later, Lincoln was sworn in as president. Afterward, he met with William in private. There is no record of what they said. But Lincoln somehow convinced William that he had an important role to play in the government, and William accepted the job in Lincoln's cabinet.

Secretary of State Seward's main job during the war was handling relations with other countries. The CSA claimed to be an independent country. They wanted other nations to recognize their independence and help them fight

The first battle of the Civil War took place at Fort Sumter when Confederate soldiers attacked and had their first victory in the harbor of Charleston, South Carolina.

the United States. William had to convince other countries that the Southern states were still part of the United States and did not deserve foreign support.

Great Britain was William's biggest concern. British factories used Southern cotton to produce cloth. Some important British leaders wanted to help the Confederacy. Great Britain never did recognize Southern independence.

Officially, Britain was **neutral**—it did not support either side in the Civil War. But the British still sometimes helped the South.

Soon after the war started, the North put a **blockade** around Southern ports. Union warships prevented ships from sailing to or from these ports. The blockade threatened to harm British trade with the South. Confederate ships had to sneak past the blockade to reach the Atlantic Ocean. The British helped the Southerners by building two ships for them. The ships were supposed to carry goods. But as soon as the ships left Great Britain, the Confederacy turned them into warships.

In November 1861, two Confederate officials on their way to Europe boarded the British ship *Trent* in Havana, Cuba. A Union warship under the command of Captain Charles Wilkes stopped the *Trent* off Cuba. Wilkes took the two Confederates as prisoners.

When news of the *Trent* affair reached the North, Wilkes was treated as a hero. Many

**The British Ambassador Lord Lyons (left) is shown
meeting with Secretary of State Seward to discuss
the *Trent* affair.**

British citizens, however, were outraged. They
believed the Americans had no right to stop a
British ship off Cuba. British leaders demanded
that the Americans apologize and release the two
Confederates. If not, Britain was ready for war.

Captain Wilkes had acted on his own, not on
government orders. After the British threat, Lincoln met with William and the rest of the cabinet.

No one wanted a war with Great Britain. William wrote a letter agreeing to release the prisoners. But the Americans did not admit that they had acted illegally by taking them.

The British had already sent troops to Canada in case war broke out with the United States. Lord Lyons was the British **ambassador** in Washington. He accepted William's note and worked with William during the *Trent* affair. Afterward, Lyons wrote that William had "worked very hard and exposed his popularity to very great danger" during the crisis. The *Trent* affair was the biggest diplomatic problem William faced early in the Civil War.

As 1861 ended, the war seemed to be growing. The first major battles had been fought in Virginia. The two sides also clashed farther west. Both sides were also building up their navies. The Civil War would not "blow over," as William had once hoped.

President Lincoln is shown reading the Emancipation Proclamation during the Civil War to members of his Cabinet in September 1862. The final proclamation was issued on January 1, 1863, and freed salves in the Confederate states that were in rebellion.

Victory and Tragedy

At the beginning of 1862, the North won several victories. William and other Northerners thought the South might be ready to discuss peace. William sent a message to the Southern leaders through the French ambassador in Washington. The ambassador returned and told William and Lincoln that the South was ready to fight on.

William continued trying to improve relations with Great Britain. He wrote a letter to Lord Lyons early in the year. "In this and in all matters," the secretary wrote, "we desire to be good friends with you, if we can." But as the year went on, relations with

Britain worsened. The South began to do better on the battlefield. These victories made both Britain and France consider recognizing the Confederacy's independence.

Around this time, more Americans were calling on Lincoln to **emancipate**, or free, the slaves in the South. Lincoln did not want to do this. He always said the war was about keeping the Union whole. But by giving Southern slaves their freedom, they could help the North fight the war. When Lincoln asked his cabinet what to do, William suggested he delay emancipation. He was not sure emancipation was the right thing to do. William thought that ending slavery so suddenly would ruin the economy in the South. If that happened, France or Britain might step in to help the Confederacy.

Finally, in September 1862, Lincoln issued his Emancipation **Proclamation**. This official statement said that all Southern slaves would be free as of January 1, 1863. The proclamation did not affect slaves in the border states that had remained in the Union. William signed the proclamation, but he still had doubts about it.

In the summer of 1863, two more Confederate ships were almost ready to be launched. They were **ironclads**–wooden ships covered with iron plates. They also had large metal rams on their fronts. These rams could easily pierce wooden Union ships. William sent a message to Charles Francis Adams, the U.S. ambassador in Great Britain. He wanted Adams to tell the British that the ships must not sail. If they did, and if they attacked Union ships, the Union would go to war with Britain.

The British had already decided to keep the ships from sailing. The problem with the ironclads soon faded. But William still had other issues with the British. At the time, Britain owned many islands in the Caribbean Sea. They also controlled Canada. The South sought help from British citizens in both areas. William continued to confront the British about this aid.

The Union also faced problems with France. Its ruler, Napoleon III, sided with the South. France needed Southern cotton. Still, like the British, the French remained mostly neutral. At times, though, the French offered some small aid to the Confederates.

William watched the French closely, as they become involved in North American affairs. In 1862, French troops landed in Mexico. Napoleon III wanted to take control of the country and put in a ruler that would be friendly to France. French troops took complete control of Mexico in the summer of 1863. Under the Monroe Doctrine of 1823, the United States said it would not let any European nation take control of a country in North or South America. During 1864, more Americans wanted the Union to put the Monroe Doctrine into action. But the United States was too busy with the Civil War to fight the French.

By now, Napoleon III had selected an emperor named Maximilian to rule Mexico.

William refused to recognize him as the ruler. Despite this, Napoleon III tried to have better relations with the Union. It was becoming clear that the North would win the Civil War. After the war, America would be able to send its troops to fight in Mexico, if necessary. The French made plans to take their army out of Mexico.

In general, William's dealings with the Europeans became easier as the North closed in on a victory. The foreign diplomats he worked with came to respect his ability. At home, Lincoln valued William as a skilled adviser on many issues. The two worked closely to end the war.

In February 1865, William and Lincoln met with representatives from the Confederacy to discuss ending the war. The North had several demands. The most important demand was that the South rejoins the Union. William and Lincoln also wanted to abolish slavery. Yet they were willing to do it slowly and let the South play a role in how it was done.

Not all of William Henry Seward's attention was focused on the Civil War. In the fall of 1863, he saw a letter sent to President Lincoln asking him to create a national holiday of thanksgiving. At the time, only some states had their own day of thanksgiving. William liked the idea, and he wrote a proclamation. He proposed that Thanksgiving come on the last Thursday in November. Americans could remember all the privileges they enjoyed, even during wartime. Lincoln used William's proclamation to create the first official Thanksgiving holiday.

The peace conference was not successful. The South chose to continue fighting. By April, however, the Confederates were doomed. On the April 9, General Robert E. Lee surrendered to Union general Ulysses S. Grant. Unfortunately for William, he could not celebrate the North's victory. A few days earlier, he had been in an accident. The horses pulling his carriage had run off, and William tried to grab their reins to stop them. Instead, he fell and broke an arm and his jaw, and William spent more than a week in bed.

The secretary was home the night of April 14, still recovering from the accident. Inside his

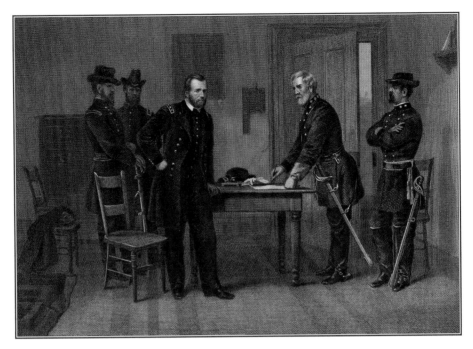

Confederate General Robert E. Lee surrendered the Army of Northern Virginia to Union General Ulysses S. Grant at Appomattox Court House, Virginia, ending the Civil War.

room, his daughter Fanny read to him as a nurse sat nearby. The three heard a noise in the hall. Fanny went out and saw her brother Frederick talking to a stranger. Fanny returned to her father's room. Moments later, they heard a gunshot. William's nurse now opened the door. The stranger was in the hallway, holding a long

Lewis Payne is shown here in chains after his assault on Secretary of State Seward. The attempt on Seward's life was part of the larger plan that also included the assassination of President Lincoln.

knife. He slashed at the nurse, then rushed over to William's bed. The man struck again, and blood poured from William's face and other cuts on his body. The stranger ran off before he could kill William.

At almost the same time, another **assassin** was more successful. President Lincoln was attending a play at Washington's Ford Theater. As Lincoln watched the play, John Wilkes Booth slipped behind the president's seat, shot Lincoln, and then fled the theater. The attacks on Lincoln and William were linked. The stranger who tried to kill William was Lewis Payne. He and Booth had worked together in this plot to kill the president and the secretary of state.

Most of Richmond, Virginia, was ruined. Union forces entered the Confederate capital and found this arsenal and the surrounding neighborhood destroyed by fire.

Last Years of Service

Slowly, William recovered from his injuries, but soon he faced another difficult time. His wife Frances had been ill for some time. The attack on William upset her so much that her health worsened. Frances Seward died in June.

A few weeks later, William was ready to return to work full time. Andrew Johnson, a Democrat, was now president. He and his cabinet had to find the best way to bring the South into the Union. They also had to find a way to deal with the end of slavery across the country. Many Southerners did not want to give African Americans legal rights, even though they were free citizens.

President Andrew Johnson's Reconstruction plan did not please everyone in the country. William agreed with most of the plan and supported Johnson's efforts.

The time after the Civil War is called the Reconstruction Era. The country had to reconstruct, or rebuild, the damaged parts of the North and South. In Washington, the Republican Party controlled the government. Some Republicans supported Johnson's plans for Reconstruction. Others, however, wanted greater legal protection for blacks. They also wanted harsh punishments for former Confederate leaders. These Republicans were called Radicals.

William supported Johnson's policies for the South. He always believed that most Southerners were loyal to the Union. With slavery abolished, William hoped to create better relations between the North and South. During the Reconstruction Era, William said he believed in "the honest and peaceful intentions of the citizens of the southern states."

William also agreed with Johnson that the Southern states should decide when African Americans could vote. "The North," he told a reporter, "has nothing to do with the negroes." Radical

Republicans disliked this opinion, and some disliked William as well. But the Radicals especially disliked Johnson and his Reconstruction. They set out their own plans for Reconstruction.

From 1865 through 1867, Johnson and the Radicals battled over the South. In 1866, Congress passed the Civil Rights Act. This law said African Americans born in the United States were citizens and had the same legal right as whites. Johnson rejected the law, but Congress had enough votes to pass it without his approval. Later Radical acts set up military control over the Southern states.

William remained loyal to Johnson, even though his own popularity suffered. During this difficult time, William struggled with another huge personal loss. Late in 1866, his daughter Fanny died, and William was crushed.

While Johnson and the Radicals battled over Reconstruction, William carried out his foreign duties. He had always wanted the United States to expand and gain new lands. Some of these lands, he believed, could help the U.S. Navy. Ships in the 1860s ran on coal. They needed to stop frequently to pick up more of this fuel. William wanted to purchase islands that could be used as coaling stations. In 1866, he made plans to buy three islands from Denmark. They were known as the Danish West Indies. Today, these islands in the Caribbean Sea are called the U.S. Virgin Islands.

William also explored buying other islands. He thought about Greenland and Iceland. He tried to improve relations with the leaders of Hawaii, hoping the island might become part of the United States some day. Most members of Congress were not interested in William's plans. A few people thought he was foolish to try to buy foreign lands. That opinion grew when William turned his attention north, to Alaska.

In the 19th century, Russia controlled Alaska. William had been interested in this land since the 1850s. He knew it had gold, timber, and other natural resources. He also knew that

Alaska could one day be important for trading with Asia. Many Americans wanted to sell goods to China and Japan, and Alaska could be a base for U.S. ships in the Pacific Ocean.

In March 1867, William signed a treaty with Russia to buy Alaska for $7.2 million. Not everyone liked the plan. Some senators did not like any idea that came from William. He and Johnson were still unpopular with the Radicals. Others said Alaska was only a land of icebergs, and the United States did not need more territory. Some people called Alaska "Seward's Folly."

The U.S. Senate had to approve the treaty that sold Alaska to the United States. William used his friends and newspapers to convince Americans that the land was valuable, and not a worthless folly. In April the Senate agreed and approved the treaty.

During William's last year in Washington, President Johnson faced a crisis. His relations with the Radical Republicans in Congress and in his cabinet had worsened. One of these was

In March 1867, William (seated, left) negotiated the treaty of purchase Alaska from Russia.

Secretary of War Edwin Stanton. Johnson wanted to fire Stanton. Congress passed a law to prevent the president from doing this. Johnson ignored the law and fired Stanton anyway. An angry Congress then decided to **impeach** Johnson.

Impeachment is a legal method to remove a government official from office. A president accused of committing a crime can be impeached. The House of Representatives accuses the president of specific crimes. Then the Senate decides if the president is innocent or guilty.

The Panama Canal links the Atlantic and Pacific Oceans and greatly shortens the voyage for ships sailing between America's two coasts. The canal opened in 1914, but William had tried to build it decades earlier.

In 1868, William found businessmen who would help build a canal. He sent a representative to talk to leaders in the South American country of Colombia, which then ruled Panama. Colombia agreed to give land to the United States for a canal. The canal would be built within 15 years. William gladly accepted this deal. But some Colombian leaders and U.S. senators rejected the plan. The United States had to wait almost 50 years for its canal.

The impeachment of Andrew Johnson began in February 1868. William had disagreed with Johnson on some parts of Reconstruction. He also did not think Johnson should have fired Stanton. But William remained loyal to the president during the impeachment. In the end, Johnson was found innocent.

By the end of the impeachment, William's career was almost over. Johnson did not run for office again in the election of 1868. The new president was General Ulysses S. Grant. Early in 1869, William resigned as secretary of state. He was

William started negotiations for the Panama Canal in 1868. His plans eventually failed, and it would take many years before the canal was finally built.

not sorry to leave political life. A friend wrote that he never saw William "more happy than he is now; so different . . . from what he has been the last ten years."

William now had time to travel, and he set off for Alaska. He traveled by train to California and then sailed northward. He also spent time in Canada and Mexico. In 1870, William began a trip around the world, though by now his health was not always good. During his travels, William visited Japan, China, India, and Egypt. He returned to Auburn, New York, late in 1871, and he began to write his autobiography. He also worked on a book about his world travels. He continued to write until the day he died, on October 10, 1872.

William Henry Seward has been called a complex man. He wanted success and power for himself, hoping to eventually serve as president. He loved his country and wanted what was best for it. William thought slavery was an evil that had to be eliminated. William is remembered today for his antislavery stance. He is also honored for his early leadership in the Republican Party and his service to America during and after the Civil War.

GLOSSARY

abolitionists–people who demand an immediate end to slavery.

ambassador–a person who represents his or her government in a foreign country.

assassin–a person who tries to kill a political leader.

blockade–the use of ships to keep ports closed.

border states–the states that allowed slavery and remained part of the Union during the Civil War.

cabinet–the heads of government departments who advise a leader.

candidate–a person running for a political office.

convention–a meeting of people with similar interests.

denizen–citizen.

emancipate–to free, especially people held as slaves.

impeach–to try to remove a government official from office.

ironclads–wooden ships covered with thick sheets of iron.

legislature–the part of an elected government that creates laws.

militia–a group of citizens who serve as soldiers during an emergency.

monarchy–a type of government ruled by a king or queen.

neutral–not favoring either side in a war.

nominated–the naming of a particular candidate to run for political office.

plantations–large farms, especially in the Southern part of the United States.

prejudice–strong feelings against something or someone.

proclamation–an official statement by a government.

radical–a person thought to have extreme beliefs on a subject.

revolt–an armed attack against people in power.

secede–break away from a country or state.

CHRONOLOGY

1801	Born May 16th in Florida, Orange County, New York.
1816	Enters Union College in Schenectady, New York.
1819	Travels to Georgia.
1820	Graduates from Union College and begins studying law.
1822	Becomes a lawyer.
1824	Marries Frances Miller.
1830	Elected to the New York state senate.
1838	Elected governor of New York and serves for four years.
1846	Defends Henry Wyatt and William Freeman, two free blacks accused of murder.
1848	Elected to the U.S. Senate.
1850	Delivers his "Higher Law" speech in the Senate.
1854	Reelected to the Senate.
1855	Joins the Republican Party and becomes one of its leaders.
1860	Loses the Republican presidential nomination to Abraham Lincoln.
1861	Becomes secretary of state under President Lincoln.
1865	Wounded as part of the assassination plot against President Lincoln.
1867	Arranges for the United States to purchase Alaska.
1869	Visits Alaska after resigning as secretary of state.
1870	Travels around the world.
1872	Dies in Auburn, New York, on October 10th.

CIVIL WAR TIME LINE

1860   Abraham Lincoln is elected president of the United States on November 6. During the next few months, Southern states begin to break away from the Union.

1861   On April 12, the Confederates attack Fort Sumter, South Carolina, and the Civil War begins. Union forces are defeated in Virginia at the First Battle of Bull Run (First Manassas) on July 21 and withdraw to Washington, D.C.

1862   Robert E. Lee is placed in command of the main Confederate army in Virginia in June. Lee defeats the Army of the Potomac at the Second Battle of Bull Run (Second Manassas) in Virginia on August 29–30. On September 17, Union general George B. McClellan turns back Lee's first invasion of the North at Antietam Creek near Sharpsburg, Maryland. It is the bloodiest day of the war.

1863   On January 1, President Lincoln issues the Emancipation Proclamation, freeing slaves in Southern states. Between May 1–6, Lee wins an important victory at Chancellorsville, but key Southern commander Thomas J. "Stonewall" Jackson dies from wounds. In June, Union forces hold the city of Vicksburg, Mississippi, under siege. The people of Vicksburg surrender on July 4. Lee's second invasion of the North during July 1–3 is decisively turned back at Gettysburg, Pennsylvania.

1864	General Grant is made supreme Union commander on March 9. Following a series of costly battles, on June 19 Grant successfully encircles Lee's troops in Petersburg, Virginia. A siege of the town lasts nearly a year.
	Union general William Sherman captures Atlanta on September 2 and begins the "March to the Sea," a campaign of destruction across Georgia and South Carolina. On November 8, Abraham Lincoln wins reelection as president.
1865	On April 2, Petersburg, Virginia, falls to the Union. Lee attempts to reach Confederate forces in North Carolina but is gradually surrounded by Union troops. Lee surrenders to Grant on April 9 at Appomattox, Virginia, ending the war. Abraham Lincoln is assassinated by John Wilkes Booth on April 14.

FURTHER READING

Cohen, Daniel. *The Alaska Purchase.* Brookfield, CT: Millbrook Press, 1996.

Dolan, Edward F. *The House Divided: The Civil War.* Brookfield, CT: Millbrook Press, 1997.

Hakim, Joy. *Reconstruction and Reform. A History of US.* Vol. 7, 2nd ed. New York: Oxford University Press, 1999.

Kent, Zachary. *William Seward: The Mastermind of the Alaska Purchase.* Berkeley Heights, NJ: Enslow Publishers, 2001.

King, Wilma. *Toward the Promised Land, 1851–1861: From Uncle Tom's Cabin to the Onset of the Civil War. Milestones in Black American History.* New York: Chelsea House , 1995.

Lutz, Norma Jean. *The History of the Republican Party.* Philadelphia: Chelsea House, 2000.

INDEX

ABOUT THE AUTHOR

MICHAEL BURGAN was an editor at Weekly Reader, where he created educational material for an interactive, online service and wrote about current events. Michael is now a freelance author and a member of the Society of Children's Book Writers and Illustrators. His books include biographies of President John F. Kennedy, Secretary of State Madeleine Albright, and astronaut John Glenn; two volumes in the series American Immigration; and short books on the Boston Tea Party, the Declaration of Independence, the Bill of Rights, and the New Deal. Michael has a BA in history from the University of Connecticut.

PICTURE CREDITS